Hymns of Hope and Songs of Assurance

Iouri Grichetchkine

Editor: Carson Cooman
Music Engraving: Lyndell Leatherman
Cover Design: Patti Jeffers

ISBN: 978-0-7877-6796-9

Copyright © 2019 Lorenz Publishing Company, a division of The Lorenz Corporation. All
rights reserved. Printed in the U.S.A. Reproduction of this publication without permission
of the publisher is a criminal offense subject to prosecution.

Lorenz

A Lorenz Company • www.lorenz.com

Foreword

Iouri Grichetchkine has crafted a set of fresh arrangements of a number of beloved classic hymns of the faith. Ranging from lyrical and expressive to rhythmic and vital, these delightful organ settings will serve as valuable material for preludes, offertories, and postludes.

Provided registrations and dynamics are only suggestions. Feel free to adapt as necessary to make the music sound its very best on your organ.

The Publisher

Contents

Be Thou My Vision

Sw. Foundations 8, 4
Gt.   Principal 8
Ped. 16, 8 to balance, Sw. to Ped.

Iouri Grichetchkine
Tune: **SLANE**
Irish melody

Duration: 3:40

© 2019 Lorenz Publishing Co., a division of the Lorenz Corporation. All rights reserved. Printed in U.S.A.
UNAUTHORIZED REPRODUCTION OF THIS PUBLICATION IS A CRIMINAL OFFENSE SUBJECT TO PROSECUTION
www.lorenz.com

LL

8

Blessed Assurance

Sw. Foundations 8, 4
Gt. Foundations 8, 4, Sw. to Gt.
Ped. 16, 8 to balance, Sw. to Ped.

Iouri Grichetchkine
Tune: ASSURANCE
by **Phoebe Palmer Knapp**

Duration: 2:30

© 2019 Lorenz Publishing Co., a division of the Lorenz Corporation. All rights reserved. Printed in U.S.A.
UNAUTHORIZED REPRODUCTION OF THIS PUBLICATION IS A CRIMINAL OFFENSE SUBJECT TO PROSECUTION
www.lorenz.com

LL

It Is Well with My Soul

Sw. Strings 8
Gt.   Flutes 8, 2, Sw. to Gt.
Ped. Flutes 16, 8

Iouri Grichetchkine
Tune: VILLE DU HAVRE
by **Philip P. Bliss**

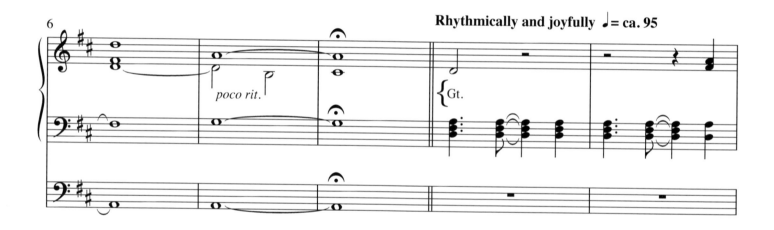

Duration: 5:40

© 2019 Lorenz Publishing Co., a division of the Lorenz Corporation. All rights reserved. Printed in U.S.A.
UNAUTHORIZED REPRODUCTION OF THIS PUBLICATION IS A CRIMINAL OFFENSE SUBJECT TO PROSECUTION
www.lorenz.com

LL

Just As I Am, Without One Plea

Sw. Foundations 8, 4
Gt. Foundations 8, 4, 2
Ped. 16, 8 to balance

Iouri Grichetchkine
Tune: WOODWORTH
by **William B. Bradbury**

Duration: 2:40

© 2019 Lorenz Publishing Co., a division of the Lorenz Corporation. All rights reserved. Printed in U.S.A.
UNAUTHORIZED REPRODUCTION OF THIS PUBLICATION IS A CRIMINAL OFFENSE SUBJECT TO PROSECUTION
www.lorenz.com

LL

24

70/2207L-24

Wonderful Words of Life

Sw. String, Celeste
Gt. Flutes 8, 4
Ped. Quiet 16, 8

Iouri Grichetchkine
Tune: WORDS OF LIFE
by **Philip P. Bliss**

Duration: 2:20

© 2019 Lorenz Publishing Co., a division of the Lorenz Corporation. All rights reserved. Printed in U.S.A.
UNAUTHORIZED REPRODUCTION OF THIS PUBLICATION IS A CRIMINAL OFFENSE SUBJECT TO PROSECUTION
www.lorenz.com

70/2207L-27

LL

O for a Thousand Tongues to Sing

Sw. Flutes and Strings 8, 4
Gt. Flutes 8, 4, Sw. to Gt.
Ped. 16, 8 to balance, Sw. to Ped.

Iouri Grichetchkine
Tune: AZMON
by **C. G. Gläser**
Adapted by **Lowell Mason**

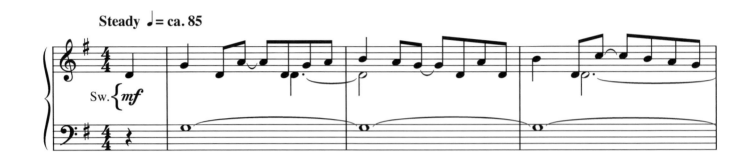

Duration: 3:00

© 2019 Lorenz Publishing Co., a division of the Lorenz Corporation. All rights reserved. Printed in U.S.A.
UNAUTHORIZED REPRODUCTION OF THIS PUBLICATION IS A CRIMINAL OFFENSE SUBJECT TO PROSECUTION
www.lorenz.com

LL

Sweet Hour of Prayer

Sw. String, Celeste, Flute
Gt. Flutes 8, 4, Sw. to Gt.
Ped. Quiet 16, 8

Iouri Grichetchkine
Tune: SWEET HOUR
by **William B. Bradbury**

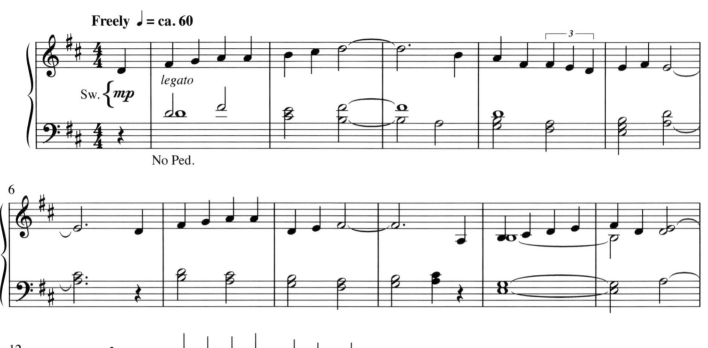

Duration: 5:30

© 2019 Lorenz Publishing Co., a division of the Lorenz Corporation. All rights reserved. Printed in U.S.A.
UNAUTHORIZED REPRODUCTION OF THIS PUBLICATION IS A CRIMINAL OFFENSE SUBJECT TO PROSECUTION
www.lorenz.com

LL

What a Friend We Have in Jesus

Sw. Flutes 8, 4
Gt. Principals 8, 4
Ped. 16, 8 to balance

Iouri Grichetchkine
Tune: CONVERSE
by Charles C. Converse

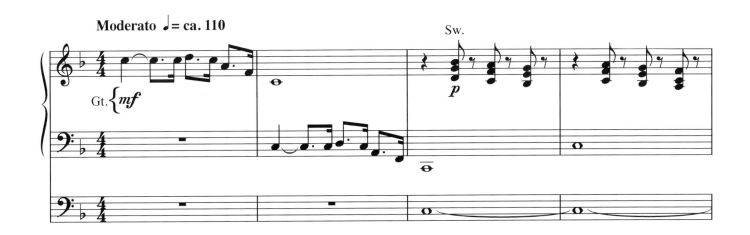

Duration: 2:30

© 2019 Lorenz Publishing Co., a division of the Lorenz Corporation. All rights reserved. Printed in U.S.A.
UNAUTHORIZED REPRODUCTION OF THIS PUBLICATION IS A CRIMINAL OFFENSE SUBJECT TO PROSECUTION
www.lorenz.com

LL

To God Be the Glory

Sw. Foundations 8, 4, 2
Gt. Foundations 8, Sw. to Gt.
Ped. 16, 8 to balance, Sw. to Ped.

Iouri Grichetchkine
Tune: TO GOD BE THE GLORY
by **William Howard Doane**

Duration: 0:00

© 2019 Lorenz Publishing Co., a division of the Lorenz Corporation. All rights reserved. Printed in U.S.A.
UNAUTHORIZED REPRODUCTION OF THIS PUBLICATION IS A CRIMINAL OFFENSE SUBJECT TO PROSECUTION
www.lorenz.com

LL

Tempo di marcia ♩ = ca. 110

52